Table of Contents

Introduction

Welcome to "The Ultimate Guide on How To: Start a Fractional CFO Business!" If you've ever dreamed of leveraging your financial expertise to help businesses thrive without committing to a full-time role, this book is for you. We're going to explore the key steps and strategies you need to establish and grow your own fractional CFO business successfully.

In today's fast-paced and ever-evolving business environment, many small and medium-sized companies recognize the value of having a fractional CFO on their team. A fractional CFO, also known as an outsourced CFO or part-time CFO, provides high-level financial expertise and guidance to businesses that may not have the resources or need for a full-time CFO.

Throughout this guide, we'll delve into every aspect of starting and running a fractional CFO business. We'll begin by defining what a fractional CFO is and the vital role they play in businesses of all sizes and industries. We'll also discuss the growing demand for fractional CFO services and the numerous benefits they offer to both clients and entrepreneurs like yourself.

To help you assess your qualifications and expertise in finance and accounting, Chapter 2 will feature self-assessment exercises. This chapter will also explore educational and professional development opportunities that can enhance your skills and help you identify your target market and niches within the fractional CFO industry.

Once you've determined your qualifications and target market, Chapter 3 will provide an in-depth understanding of the responsibilities and duties of a fractional CFO. We will discuss the immense value a fractional CFO can bring to businesses and offer tips on positioning yourself as a trusted advisor and strategic partner to your clients.

Chapter 4 will cover the practical steps of setting up your fractional CFO business. This includes registering your business, obtaining the necessary licenses, selecting accounting software and tools, and creating professional branding and marketing materials to establish your credibility in the industry.

In Chapter 5, we'll dive into strategies for building your client base. We'll discuss techniques such as networking, referrals, and utilizing online platforms to market your services effectively. We'll also provide tips on creating compelling proposals and presentations to win clients over and stand out from the competition.

Once you've acquired clients, Chapter 6 will guide you on how to provide exceptional fractional CFO services. We'll explore best practices for assessing clients' financial needs, developing customized solutions, and effectively managing financial reporting, budgeting, forecasting, and strategic planning.

Chapter 7 will focus on pricing your fractional CFO services. We'll help you determine the factors to consider when setting your pricing structure and provide various pricing models and strategies to ensure competitiveness and profitability. We'll also offer advice on communicating your value to clients and effectively negotiating pricing agreements.

Managing your fractional CFO business will be the subject of Chapter 8. We'll discuss setting up systems and processes to manage workflow, client communications, and deadlines. Plus, we'll provide tips for staying organized and maintaining accurate records for your own business, as well as strategies for effectively managing finances, expenses, and cash flow.

As your business grows, Chapter 9 will outline strategies for scaling your fractional CFO business. We'll explore opportunities for expansion, including outsourcing tasks to increase your efficiency and exploring new avenues for growth and diversification.

Finally, in Chapter 10, we will address the challenges that you may encounter as a fractional CFO and provide strategies for overcoming them. We'll emphasize the importance of staying updated on industry trends, regulations, and best practices, as well as maintaining strong client relationships and managing your workload to sustain long-term success.

Through this comprehensive guide, we aim to equip you with the knowledge and tools needed to start and thrive in your own fractional CFO business. So, let's begin this enriching journey together and turn your entrepreneurial dreams into a reality!

Chapter 1: Introduction to Fractional CFO Services

Fractional CFO services have become a game-changer in the business world, offering a cost-effective solution for companies that need high-level financial expertise without the full-time commitment. In this chapter, we'll explore what a fractional CFO does, why their services are in growing demand, and the benefits they can provide to businesses. Additionally, we'll give you a roadmap of what to expect in this guide, ensuring you're equipped with all the knowledge needed to dive into this exciting field.

Defining the Fractional CFO Role

A fractional CFO, also known as an outsourced CFO or part-time CFO, is a financial professional who provides strategic financial guidance and support to businesses on a part-time or as-needed basis. Unlike a full-time CFO who is dedicated to a single company, a fractional CFO works with multiple clients, offering their expertise across different industries and business sizes.

The role of a fractional CFO extends beyond traditional accounting tasks. They are instrumental in helping businesses make informed financial decisions, optimize operations, and achieve financial goals. Working closely with business owners, executives, and management teams, fractional CFOs provide critical financial insights, develop strategies, and enhance overall financial performance. Their work is crucial for steering businesses towards sustainable growth and profitability.

The Growing Demand for Fractional CFO Services

In recent years, the demand for fractional CFO services has surged. Small and medium-sized businesses often lack the resources to hire a full-time CFO but still require seasoned financial guidance to navigate complex financial landscapes. This is where fractional CFOs step in, offering their expertise on a flexible basis that suits the specific needs and budgets of these businesses.

Startups and entrepreneurial ventures, in particular, benefit greatly from fractional CFOs. These companies may not have the financial means to employ a full-time CFO but still need strategic financial advice to fuel growth and secure funding. By hiring a fractional CFO, they gain access to high-level financial expertise without incurring the costs associated with a permanent CFO position.

The Benefits of Fractional CFO Services

There are numerous benefits for businesses utilizing fractional CFO services:

Cost-Effectiveness

Fractional CFOs provide a budget-friendly alternative to hiring a full-time CFO. Companies save on salary expenses, benefits, and overhead costs while still receiving top-tier financial expertise.

Fresh Perspective

Working with multiple clients across various industries, fractional CFOs bring a broad knowledge base and diverse experience. They can apply best practices from different contexts to offer innovative solutions and strategic insights, driving growth and improving financial performance.

Flexibility and Scalability

Fractional CFOs offer unmatched flexibility and scalability. They can adapt to changing business needs, whether during periods of growth, capital raising, or financial restructuring. Businesses can scale their engagement with a fractional CFO up or down as required, providing maximum flexibility without the long-term commitment of a full-time hire.

Outline of the Guide

In this guide, we will delve deep into the world of fractional CFO services, equipping entrepreneurs with the knowledge and tools needed to start their own successful fractional CFO business. Here's what we'll cover:

- **Assessing Your Skills and Experience:** Understanding what it takes to be a successful fractional CFO.
- **Understanding the Role:** A detailed look at the responsibilities and impact of a fractional CFO.
- **Setting Up Your Business:** Steps to establish your own fractional CFO practice.
- **Building a Client Base:** Strategies for attracting and retaining clients.
- **Providing Exceptional Services:** Best practices for delivering outstanding financial guidance.
- **Pricing Your Services:** How to set competitive and profitable rates.
- **Managing Your Business:** Effective management practices to ensure smooth operations.

- **Scaling Your Operations:** Strategies for growing your business and expanding your services.
- **Navigating Challenges:** Tips for overcoming common obstacles and sustaining long-term success.

By the end of this guide, you will have a comprehensive understanding of the fractional CFO industry and the steps required to establish and grow your own successful fractional CFO business. So let's dive into the details and embark on this exciting entrepreneurial journey together.

Chapter 2: Assessing Your Skills and Experience

Starting a fractional CFO business is no small feat. It requires a robust foundation in finance and accounting. Before diving headfirst into this venture, it's essential to take a step back and assess your skills and expertise in these areas. Conducting a self-assessment will help you identify your strengths, weaknesses, and areas where you might need some improvement. Here are some exercises to help you get started:

Self-Assessment Exercises to Determine Your Qualifications and Expertise

Evaluate Your Educational Background:

1. Start by considering your academic qualifications in finance and accounting. Did you earn a degree in these fields? Reflect on the knowledge and skills you acquired during your education. Do you have a solid understanding of financial concepts and principles? This

foundational knowledge is crucial for a successful fractional CFO career.

Analyze Your Professional Experience:

2. Next, take stock of your work experience. Have you held financial roles in the past? Evaluate the depth and breadth of your experience. What types of tasks have you handled? What industries have you worked in? Understanding your professional journey will help you recognize where you excel and where you might need further development.

Assess Your Technical Skills:

3. Modern fractional CFOs rely on a variety of software and tools to perform their duties efficiently. Evaluate your proficiency with accounting software, financial modeling tools, and other relevant technologies. Are there any gaps in your technical skills? If so, consider acquiring the necessary training or certifications to fill these gaps.

Reflect on Your Analytical Abilities:

4. Being a fractional CFO requires strong analytical skills. Consider your ability to analyze financial data, identify trends, and make sound recommendations based on the information at hand. Assess your critical thinking skills, problem-solving abilities, and attention to detail. These skills are essential for making informed financial decisions and providing valuable insights to clients.

Exploring Educational and Professional Development Opportunities to Enhance Your Skills

Once you have a clear understanding of your current skills and have identified areas for improvement, it's time to explore educational and professional development opportunities. Here are some avenues to consider:

Enroll in Relevant Courses or Certifications:

1. Look for courses or certifications that can enhance your knowledge and skills in finance and accounting. Consider programs offered by reputable institutions or professional

organizations. Some examples include Certified Public Accountant (CPA) courses, financial modeling courses, or executive education programs focused on finance and strategy.

Attend Industry Conferences and Seminars:

2. Participating in industry conferences, seminars, and workshops can provide valuable insights into the latest trends and practices in finance and accounting. These events also offer excellent networking opportunities to connect with industry experts and potential clients.

Join Professional Associations and Networks:

3. Getting involved in professional associations and networks specific to the finance and accounting industry can provide access to resources, mentorship, and networking opportunities. Consider joining organizations such as the Financial Planning Association (FPA) or the Institute of Management Accountants (IMA).

Seek Mentorship and Guidance:

4. Connect with experienced professionals in the fractional CFO industry who can offer guidance and mentorship. Their insights and advice can help you navigate the challenges and complexities of starting and growing your business.

Tips for Identifying Your Target Market and Niches Within the Fractional CFO Industry

Identifying your target market is crucial for the success of your fractional CFO business. It helps you focus your efforts on a specific group of clients and allows you to tailor your services to meet their unique needs. Here are some tips for identifying your target market and finding niches within the fractional CFO industry:

Research Different Industries:

1. Explore various industries and assess their specific financial needs. Consider the challenges and pain points they face and evaluate whether your expertise aligns with their requirements. You may find that certain industries, such as

healthcare or technology, have a higher demand for fractional CFO services.

Define Your Ideal Client Profile:

2. Create a profile of your ideal client based on factors such as company size, revenue, industry, and growth stage. This will help you narrow down your target market and focus your marketing efforts more effectively.

Consider Geographic Location:

3. Evaluate whether you want to serve clients locally, regionally, or nationally. Some fractional CFO businesses prefer to work with clients in their immediate vicinity, while others are comfortable working remotely and serving clients across different locations.

Identify Niches Within the Fractional CFO Industry:

4. While it is essential to have a broad understanding of finance and accounting, consider specializing in specific areas or industries within the fractional CFO space. This can help you

differentiate yourself from competitors and position yourself as an expert in a particular niche.

By assessing your skills and experience, exploring educational opportunities, and identifying your target market and niches within the fractional CFO industry, you can lay a solid foundation for your business's success. Taking these steps will ensure that you are well-prepared to meet the demands of your clients and excel in your new venture.

Chapter 3: Understanding the Role of a Fractional CFO

In this chapter, we're going to dive deep into the responsibilities and duties of a fractional CFO, as well as the immense value they bring to businesses across various industries. We'll also share tips on how to position yourself as a trusted advisor and strategic partner to your clients, helping you stand out in this competitive field.

Overview of the Responsibilities and Duties of a Fractional CFO

A fractional CFO plays a pivotal role in the financial management of a business. Their work goes beyond traditional accounting tasks, providing strategic financial insights that help businesses make informed decisions. Here's a closer look at what a fractional CFO does:

Financial Analysis and Reporting:

A fractional CFO is responsible for analyzing financial data, preparing financial statements, and generating reports that offer insights into the financial health of a business. They identify trends, risks, and opportunities, and provide actionable recommendations for improvement.

Budgeting and Forecasting:

Fractional CFOs assist businesses in developing budgets and financial forecasts. They collaborate with various departments to set financial goals, allocate resources, and monitor performance against targets. They also assess the financial feasibility of new projects and initiatives.

Cash Flow Management:

Effective cash flow management is crucial for any business. Fractional CFOs monitor cash inflows and outflows, optimize working capital, and implement strategies to improve liquidity. They also provide guidance on managing debt and financing options.

Financial Strategy and Planning:

Fractional CFOs work closely with business owners and executives to develop and execute financial strategies. They assess the financial implications of business decisions, evaluate investment opportunities, and provide recommendations to drive growth and profitability.

Risk Management:

Identifying and mitigating financial risks is a key responsibility of a fractional CFO. They implement internal controls, ensure compliance with regulations, and develop risk management strategies to protect the financial well-being of the company.

The Value of a Fractional CFO for Businesses

Fractional CFOs bring tremendous value to businesses, regardless of their size or industry. Here are some of the benefits they offer:

Cost-Effectiveness:

Hiring a full-time CFO can be expensive, especially for small and medium-sized businesses. Fractional CFO services offer a cost-effective alternative, providing high-level expertise on a part-time basis and reducing overhead costs.

Fresh Perspective:

Fractional CFOs bring a fresh set of eyes to a business. They offer objective insights and unbiased advice, challenging existing practices and identifying opportunities for improvement. Their external perspective can lead to innovative financial strategies and improved decision-making.

Expertise and Experience:

Fractional CFOs typically have extensive experience in finance and accounting. They bring a wealth of knowledge and expertise to help businesses navigate complex financial challenges and make strategic decisions. Their industry-specific insights can be invaluable in driving growth and profitability.

Flexibility:

Fractional CFOs offer flexibility in terms of working hours and the duration of engagement. They can adapt to the needs of the business, whether it requires short-term projects or ongoing support. This flexibility allows businesses to access financial expertise without long-term commitments.

Tips for Positioning Yourself as a Trusted Advisor and Strategic Partner

To establish yourself as a trusted advisor and strategic partner to your clients, consider the following tips:

Understand Your Clients' Businesses:

Take the time to deeply understand your clients' goals, challenges, and industry dynamics. This will enable you to provide tailored solutions and demonstrate your value as an advisor who understands their unique needs.

Communicate Effectively:

Develop strong communication skills to convey complex financial information to non-financial stakeholders. Use simple and concise language, and actively listen to your clients' concerns and questions. Build trust by being responsive and transparent.

Demonstrate Your Expertise:

Continuously invest in professional development to enhance your skills and stay updated with industry trends. Share your knowledge through thought leadership articles, blog posts, or speaking engagements. Position yourself as a subject matter expert in your field.

Build Relationships:

Cultivate strong relationships with your clients by taking a proactive approach. Provide insights and recommendations even when they may not directly relate to your contracted services. Show genuine interest in their success and offer support beyond financial matters.

Be a Problem-Solver:

Instead of just identifying issues, focus on providing solutions. Take a proactive approach to problem-solving and help your clients navigate through financial challenges. This will position you as a valuable and trusted partner who adds tangible value to their business.

By understanding the role of a fractional CFO, recognizing the value they bring to businesses, and positioning yourself as a trusted advisor, you will be able to establish a strong foundation for your fractional CFO business. Providing exceptional financial expertise and strategic insights will set you apart from the competition and ensure long-term success.

In the next chapter, we'll cover the practical steps of setting up your fractional CFO business, including business registration, obtaining necessary licenses, and creating professional branding materials. Let's continue this journey to set you on the path to success!

Chapter 4: Setting Up Your Fractional CFO Business

Starting a fractional CFO business requires careful planning and organization. In this chapter, we'll provide you with step-by-step instructions to set up your fractional CFO business successfully. We'll cover essential aspects such as business registration and licensing, selecting accounting software and tools, and creating professional branding and marketing materials. By following these strategies, you can streamline your operations, attract clients, and establish a strong foundation for your business.

Step 1: Business Registration and Licensing

The first step in setting up your fractional CFO business is to register your business and obtain any necessary licenses. Here are some key considerations:

1. Determine the Legal Structure of Your Business

Decide whether you want to operate as a sole proprietorship, partnership, or limited liability company (LLC). Each option has its own implications regarding liability, taxation, and administrative requirements. It's wise to consult with a legal professional to understand the benefits and drawbacks of each structure and choose the one that best suits your needs.

2. Register Your Business Name

Choosing a unique and memorable name for your fractional CFO business is crucial. Make sure your chosen name reflects your professionalism and expertise. Conduct a thorough search to ensure the name isn't already in use by another entity. Once you've settled on a name, register it with the appropriate local or state authorities.

3. Obtain Necessary Licenses and Permits

Research the licensing requirements for providing financial services in your jurisdiction. This might include specific certifications or permits needed to operate legally. Ensure you comply with all regulations to avoid legal issues down the line.

4. Consult with an Accountant

Seek guidance from an accountant or financial advisor to ensure compliance with tax regulations. They can help you understand the financial implications of operating your business, set up your accounting system, and advise you on tax planning and reporting.

Step 2: Selecting Accounting Software and Tools

Efficient and reliable accounting software is vital for managing the financial aspects of your fractional CFO business. Consider the following tips when selecting accounting software and tools:

1. Identify Your Needs

Evaluate your business requirements, such as financial reporting, budgeting, and forecasting. Determine the features and functionalities you need in accounting software to meet these needs.

2. Research Available Options

Look into different accounting software options and compare their features, pricing, and compatibility with your existing systems. User-friendly interfaces and robust reporting capabilities are essential.

3. Consider Cloud-Based Solutions

Cloud-based accounting software offers significant advantages, such as accessibility from anywhere and easy collaboration with clients. It also reduces the need for extensive IT infrastructure, making it a cost-effective solution.

4. Seek Recommendations

Consult with other fractional CFOs or accounting professionals for their recommendations on reliable accounting software. Reading online reviews can also provide insights into real user experiences and help you make an informed decision.

Step 3: Creating Professional Branding and Marketing Materials

To attract clients and establish credibility, it's important to invest in professional branding and marketing materials. Here are some strategies to consider:

1. Develop a Brand Identity

Create a logo and choose a consistent color palette and visual style that aligns with your business's identity. This cohesive brand image will help establish your professional presence.

2. Build a Professional Website

Your website will serve as the virtual storefront for your business. Ensure it's visually appealing, easy to navigate, and provides clear information about your services and expertise. Include client testimonials and case studies to build trust.

3. Craft Compelling Content

Create informative and engaging content on your website, blog, or social media platforms. Offering valuable insights and demonstrating your expertise will attract potential clients. Regularly updating your content keeps your audience engaged and improves your search engine rankings.

4. Network and Attend Industry Events

Attend networking events, industry conferences, and seminars to connect with potential clients and build relationships. Joining relevant professional associations or organizations can expand your network further.

5. Leverage Online Platforms

Utilize online platforms such as LinkedIn, Twitter, and Facebook to showcase your expertise and connect with your target audience. Share valuable content and engage in discussions to establish yourself as an industry thought leader.

By following these steps, you can lay a strong foundation for your fractional CFO business. Setting up your business correctly from the start will help you attract clients and operate efficiently. In the next chapter, we'll dive into techniques for finding and attracting clients for your business. Let's continue this journey together and ensure your business thrives in

the competitive world of fractional CFO
services!

Chapter 5: Building Your Client Base

Let's dive into the exciting yet challenging task of building your client base for your fractional CFO business. A solid client base is the backbone of your business's success and growth. We'll explore various techniques and strategies for finding and attracting clients, emphasizing the importance of networking, utilizing referrals, and leveraging online platforms to market your services. Additionally, we'll provide tips on creating compelling proposals and presentations to win over potential clients.

Techniques for Finding and Attracting Clients

When you're starting out, it's essential to be proactive in finding and attracting clients. Here are some techniques that can help you on this journey:

Conduct Market Research:

1. Begin by understanding your target market. Identify the industries and sectors that can benefit the most from your fractional CFO expertise. Dive deep into their specific financial

challenges and tailor your services to meet their needs. This understanding will not only help you position your services effectively but also demonstrate your commitment to solving their unique problems.

Develop an Ideal Client Profile:

2. Create a detailed profile of your ideal client. Consider factors such as industry, company size, revenue, and geographic location. This profile will help you narrow down your target market, making your marketing efforts more focused and efficient.

Networking:

3. Networking is a powerful tool in building your client base. Attend industry conferences, trade shows, and networking events to connect with potential clients. Establish relationships with professionals in related fields, such as lawyers, consultants, and accountants, who can refer clients to you. These connections can be invaluable sources of new business.

Utilize Referrals:

4. Your existing network and client base are gold mines for referrals. Encourage satisfied clients to refer your services to others by offering incentives or referral programs. Word-of-mouth referrals often carry more weight and can be a valuable source of new business.

Online Platforms:

5. Establish a strong online presence. Create a professional website and maintain active profiles on social media platforms like LinkedIn and Twitter. Regularly share valuable content, engage with your audience, and showcase your expertise. An effective online presence can attract potential clients and build your credibility.

Tips for Creating Compelling Proposals and Presentations

Winning clients involves more than just marketing your services. You need to effectively communicate your expertise and value proposition. Here are some tips for creating compelling proposals and presentations:

Tailor Your Approach:

1. Customize your proposals and presentations to address the specific needs and challenges of each potential client. Demonstrate your understanding of their business, industry, and goals. Explain how your services can address their unique financial needs, making your proposal more relevant and appealing.

Highlight Your Expertise:

2. Clearly communicate your experience, qualifications, and accomplishments. Build credibility and trust by showcasing your expertise in financial analysis, budgeting, forecasting, and strategic planning. Share case studies or success stories that highlight your previous achievements, giving potential clients confidence in your abilities.

Use Visuals:

3. Incorporate visuals like charts, graphs, and infographics to present complex financial information in an easy-to-understand and visually appealing way. Visual aids can help

clients grasp the value of your services more effectively.

Focus on Benefits:

4. Rather than just listing the features of your services, emphasize the benefits and outcomes that clients can expect from working with you. Explain how hiring a fractional CFO can save them time and money, and provide valuable financial insights that drive business growth. This benefit-focused approach can make your proposal more persuasive.

Clearly Outline Deliverables:

5. Define the scope of your services and specify the deliverables clients can expect. Clear deliverables help manage client expectations and establish a solid foundation for the client relationship, reducing the risk of misunderstandings and ensuring a smoother collaboration.

By implementing these techniques and following these tips, you can build a strong client base for your fractional CFO business. Remember to continuously refine your marketing strategies and adapt to changing market trends to ensure ongoing success. Building a client base takes time and effort, but with the right approach, you can achieve lasting growth and success for your business.

Chapter 6: Providing Exceptional Fractional CFO Services

In this chapter, we will explore how to deliver outstanding fractional CFO services to your clients. As a fractional CFO, your role transcends managing financial tasks; you are a trusted advisor and strategic partner. By helping businesses make informed financial decisions and achieve their goals, you can build strong, lasting relationships with your clients. Let's delve into best practices and effective strategies for providing exceptional service.

Assessing Clients' Financial Needs and Developing Customized Solutions

To deliver top-notch fractional CFO services, it's crucial to understand your clients' financial needs thoroughly. Here are some best practices to assess their needs and develop tailored solutions:

1. Conduct a Thorough Analysis

Begin by analyzing your clients' financial statements, cash flow, and overall financial performance. Identify areas for improvement and potential risks. This comprehensive analysis will provide a solid foundation for your strategic recommendations.

2. Understand Their Goals

Meet with your clients to understand their short-term and long-term financial goals. This insight will help you tailor your services and strategies to align with their specific objectives, ensuring that your efforts are focused and relevant.

3. Identify Pain Points

Listen attentively to your clients' concerns and challenges. Identifying areas where they need support and guidance is essential for providing effective solutions that address their specific issues.

4. Develop a Customized Plan

Based on your analysis and understanding of your clients' goals, create a customized plan that outlines the steps needed to achieve financial stability and growth. This plan should be detailed and actionable, providing a clear roadmap for your clients to follow.

5. Regularly Review and Adjust

Monitor your clients' progress and regularly review their financials. Adjust your strategies as necessary to ensure they stay on track toward their goals. Continuous evaluation and flexibility are key to maintaining alignment with your clients' evolving needs.

Managing Financial Reporting, Budgeting, Forecasting, and Strategic Planning

As a fractional CFO, you will handle crucial financial tasks such as reporting, budgeting, forecasting, and strategic planning. Here are some tips to manage these responsibilities effectively:

1. Financial Reporting

Ensure accurate and timely financial reporting. Use advanced accounting software and tools to streamline the process and provide your clients with clear, comprehensive reports. Transparency and accuracy are vital for building trust and credibility.

2. Budgeting

Work closely with your clients to create realistic budgets that align with their goals. Monitor their actual expenses and revenue against the budget, providing valuable insights to help them stay on track. Effective budgeting is essential for financial stability and growth.

3. Forecasting
Use historical data and market trends to forecast future financial performance. Help your clients anticipate potential challenges or opportunities, and develop strategies to mitigate risks and capitalize on opportunities. Proactive forecasting enables informed decision-making.

4. Strategic Planning
Collaborate with your clients to develop strategic financial plans that align with their long-term goals. Regularly review and adjust these plans based on changing circumstances to ensure they remain relevant and effective.

Strategies for Communicating Effectively with Clients and Providing Exceptional Customer Service

Effective communication and exceptional customer service are crucial for building strong relationships with your clients. Here are some strategies to enhance your communication skills and deliver outstanding customer service:

1. Active Listening

Listen attentively to your clients' concerns and questions. Take the time to fully understand their needs before providing solutions or advice. Active listening builds trust and demonstrates that you value their input.

2. Clear and Concise Communication

Communicate financial information in a way that is easy for your clients to understand, regardless of their financial background. Avoid jargon and use clear, concise language. Your goal is to make complex information accessible and actionable.

3. Regular Updates

Keep your clients informed about their financials and any relevant industry updates. Provide regular reports and updates to ensure transparency and foster trust. Consistent communication reinforces your role as a reliable partner.

4. Responsiveness

Be responsive to your clients' inquiries and concerns. Aim to address their needs promptly and efficiently. Timely responses demonstrate your commitment to their success and build confidence in your services.

5. Proactive Advice

Your expertise and experience allow you to offer proactive advice to your clients. Anticipate potential financial challenges or opportunities and provide valuable insights to help them make informed decisions. Proactive advice positions you as a strategic partner, not just a service provider.

By following these best practices and strategies, you can provide exceptional fractional CFO services that go beyond traditional accounting tasks. Your expertise, customized solutions, and exceptional customer service will position you as a trusted advisor and strategic partner to your clients, ultimately contributing to the success and growth of their businesses.

In the next chapter, we will explore techniques for finding and attracting clients for your fractional CFO business. Let's continue this journey together and ensure your business thrives in the competitive world of financial services!

Chapter 7: Pricing Your Fractional CFO Services

Determining the right pricing structure for your fractional CFO services is crucial for the success of your business. Let's explore the factors to consider when setting your pricing, different pricing models and strategies to ensure profitability and competitiveness, and techniques to effectively communicate the value of your services to clients and negotiate pricing agreements.

Factors to Consider

When determining the pricing structure for your fractional CFO services, there are several key factors to take into account:

Experience and Expertise:

1. Your level of experience and expertise in financial management and strategic planning should be reflected in your pricing. Clients are willing to pay more for a fractional CFO with a proven track record and a deep understanding of their industry. Highlight your accomplishments and specialized knowledge to justify higher rates.

Market Demand:

2. The demand for fractional CFO services in your target market will influence your pricing. If there is high demand and limited competition, you can charge higher rates. Conversely, if the market is saturated with fractional CFOs, you may need to adjust your pricing strategy to remain competitive.

Scope of Services:

3. The range and complexity of the services you offer will impact your pricing. Consider the specific financial tasks you will handle for clients, such as financial reporting, budgeting, forecasting, and strategic planning. The more comprehensive your services, the higher your pricing may be. Ensure that your pricing reflects the value and breadth of your offerings.

Time Commitment:

4. Assess the time you will dedicate to each client and project. If you anticipate spending substantial time and effort on a particular engagement, it may be necessary to adjust your pricing

accordingly. Ensure that your rates compensate for the time and expertise you bring to each project.

Overhead Costs:

5. Take into account the overhead costs associated with running your business, such as office space, software subscriptions, and professional insurance. These costs should be factored into your pricing to ensure profitability. Your rates should cover these expenses while still providing a reasonable profit margin.

Pricing Models and Strategies

There are various pricing models and strategies you can consider when setting your rates:

Hourly Rate:

1. Charging an hourly rate is a common approach for fractional CFOs. Determine your desired hourly rate based on your financial goals and the factors mentioned earlier. Be transparent with clients about your billing process and provide detailed invoices to maintain trust and

transparency. Clearly communicate how you track your time and the value clients receive for each hour billed.

Project-Based Pricing:

2. Instead of charging by the hour, you can offer fixed pricing for specific projects or engagements. This allows clients to know the total cost upfront and can be more appealing for budget-conscious clients. However, be sure to account for any potential scope creep to ensure profitability. Clearly define the project scope and deliverables to avoid misunderstandings.

Retainer Model:

3. Some fractional CFOs work on a retainer basis, where clients pay a predetermined monthly or quarterly fee for ongoing services. This model provides stability and a recurring revenue stream. Determine your retainer rate based on an estimation of the average time commitment and value provided to the client. This model fosters long-term relationships and provides clients with consistent support.

Value-Based Pricing:

4. Consider pricing your services based on the value you deliver to clients. This approach involves assessing the potential financial impact of your services on a client's business and charging accordingly. Demonstrating the tangible benefits and return on investment can justify higher prices. Highlight how your expertise will directly contribute to the client's financial success.

Communicating Value and Negotiating Pricing Agreements

Effectively communicating the value of your fractional CFO services is essential to justify your pricing to clients. Here are some techniques to help you:

Develop a Value Proposition:

1. Clearly articulate the unique benefits and advantages clients can expect from your services. Highlight how you can help them achieve their financial and business goals, improve efficiency, enhance decision-making, or mitigate risks. Your value proposition should

resonate with the client's specific needs and demonstrate your unique strengths.

Tailor Your Proposal:

2. Customize your proposal and pricing presentation to each potential client. Demonstrate your understanding of their specific needs and challenges and how your services can address them. Show real-life examples and success stories to showcase the value you have provided to similar clients. Personalization shows clients that you are invested in their success.

Offer Different Pricing Tiers:

3. Consider offering different pricing tiers with varying levels of service and benefits. This allows clients to choose the option that best fits their budget and needs while still providing opportunities for upselling and higher-priced packages. Different tiers can cater to a range of client budgets and service requirements.

Be Prepared to Negotiate:

4. Pricing negotiations are common in business. Be open to discussing pricing with potential clients while remaining firm on the value you provide. Look for win-win solutions that satisfy both parties' interests. Consider offering initial discounts or incentives to secure long-term engagements. Flexibility in negotiations can help close deals without compromising on the value you deliver.

By taking into account the factors discussed, choosing the right pricing model, and effectively communicating your value proposition, you can establish fair and competitive pricing for your fractional CFO services. Remember to regularly review and adjust your pricing strategies as your business grows and market conditions change. Keeping a pulse on market trends and client feedback will help you stay competitive and profitable in the long run.

Chapter 8: Managing Your Fractional CFO Business

Managing your fractional CFO business effectively is crucial for maintaining smooth operations, meeting client expectations, and ensuring long-term success. In this chapter, we will discuss essential strategies and tips for managing various aspects of your business, including workflow, client communications, deadlines, organization, record-keeping, and financial management.

Setting up Systems and Processes

To manage the workflow of your fractional CFO business efficiently, it's important to establish clear systems and processes. This ensures that tasks are completed on time, communication is streamlined, and deadlines are met. Here are some key steps to consider:

1. Define key processes: Identify the core processes in your business, such as client onboarding, financial reporting, budgeting, forecasting, and strategic planning. Document these processes step-by-step to create a standard operating procedure (SOP) for each.

2. Use project management tools: Invest in project management software or cloud-based platforms to help you organize tasks, assign deadlines, and collaborate with clients and team members. Tools like Asana, Trello, or Monday.com can streamline your workflow and keep everyone accountable.

3. Set clear expectations: Clearly communicate expectations and timelines to your clients. Establish deadlines for deliverables and ensure that both parties are on the same page regarding the scope of work and project milestones.

4. Develop effective communication channels: Establish a communication plan with your clients to ensure regular updates and address any concerns or questions promptly. Use a combination of email, phone calls, and video conferences to stay connected and maintain strong relationships.

Tips for Staying Organized

Maintaining organization is essential for running a successful fractional CFO business. Here are some tips to help you stay organized:

1. Use a task management system: Implement a task management system to keep track of your to-do list and prioritize tasks based on their urgency and importance. This can help you stay focused and ensure that important deadlines are met.

2. Create a filing system: Establish a structured filing system for both digital and physical documents. Organize your files in a logical manner, making it easy to locate and retrieve important information when needed.

3. Adopt a calendar tool: Utilize a calendar tool, such as Google Calendar or Microsoft Outlook, to schedule and manage your appointments, meetings, and deadlines. Set reminders to stay on top of your commitments.

4. Regularly declutter your workspace: A clutter-free workspace promotes productivity and reduces distractions. Clean and organize your physical workspace regularly to maintain a clear mind and efficient work environment.

Strategies for Managing Finances, Expenses, and Cash Flow

Managing your finances effectively is crucial for the success of your fractional CFO business. Here are some strategies to consider:

1. Create a budget: Develop a comprehensive budget that includes all anticipated expenses, such as office rent, software subscriptions, marketing costs, and professional development. Regularly review and update your budget to ensure financial stability.

2. Monitor expenses: Keep track of your expenses and regularly review them to identify areas where you can reduce costs or allocate resources more efficiently. This will help you maximize profitability and maintain a healthy cash flow.

3. Implement financial software: Consider using accounting software, such as QuickBooks or Xero, to streamline your financial management processes. This software can help you track income, expenses, and invoices, as well as generate financial reports.

4. Invoice promptly and follow up on payments: Send out invoices promptly after completing services and regularly follow up on outstanding payments. Implement a system for tracking invoices and ensure that your clients are aware of your payment terms and deadlines.

Conclusion

Managing your fractional CFO business effectively requires setting up systems and processes, staying organized, and effectively managing your finances. By implementing these strategies, you can streamline your workflow, maintain strong client relationships, and ensure the long-term success of your business.

Chapter 9: Scaling Your Fractional CFO Business

Scaling your fractional CFO business is a crucial step towards increasing revenue and achieving long-term success. In this chapter, we will explore strategies for expanding your business, outsourcing critical tasks, and diversifying your services to seize new growth opportunities. By implementing these strategies, you can take your fractional CFO business to new heights and serve a broader client base.

1. Strategies for Expanding Your Fractional CFO Business

Expanding your fractional CFO business requires careful planning and execution. Here are some strategies to consider:

a. Build Strategic Partnerships

Collaborating with other professionals, such as accountants, lawyers, and business consultants, can help you reach a wider audience and tap into new markets. Explore potential partnerships that align with your services and values, and create mutually beneficial relationships with these professionals. These alliances can provide referrals, share resources, and offer additional expertise to enhance your services.

b. Leverage Technology

Investing in technology can significantly enhance your scalability. Adopt accounting software, data analytics tools, and project management systems to streamline your operations and improve efficiency. Embracing cloud-based solutions provides flexibility and accessibility for both you and your clients. Modern technology can automate repetitive tasks, reduce errors, and allow you to focus on higher-value activities.

c. Expand Your Geographic Reach

Consider expanding your services beyond your local area. With technology enabling remote work, you can now serve clients from various locations. Conduct market research to identify regions with a high demand for fractional CFO services and tailor your marketing efforts accordingly. Expanding your geographic reach allows you to tap into new markets and diversify your client base.

2. Outsourcing Tasks to Scale Your Operations

As your business grows, it may become challenging to handle all tasks on your own. Outsourcing certain functions can help you scale your operations effectively. Here are some tasks you can consider outsourcing:

a. Bookkeeping

Outsourcing bookkeeping tasks can free up your time to focus on higher-value strategic activities. Look for reputable bookkeeping services or hire freelance bookkeepers to handle transaction recording, reconciliation, and financial statement preparation. This ensures accuracy and efficiency in managing financial records.

b. Tax Preparation

Tax preparation can be complex and time-consuming. Consider partnering with tax professionals or tax preparation firms to ensure compliance and accuracy with your clients' tax obligations. Outsourcing this task allows you to leverage specialized expertise and minimize the risk of errors.

c. Financial Analysis

Outsourcing financial analysis tasks can provide you with additional expertise and support. Collaborate with financial analysts or data analysts to help you interpret financial data, identify trends, and provide insightful recommendations to your clients. This enhances the depth and quality of the financial insights you offer.

3. Diversifying Your Services for Growth

Diversifying your services can help you attract a broader client base and increase revenue streams. Here are some ways to diversify your offerings:

a. Additional Consulting Services

Consider expanding your service offerings beyond traditional CFO responsibilities. Offer consulting services in areas such as mergers and acquisitions, business valuation, risk management, or financial planning. This expansion can position you as a comprehensive financial advisor and open doors to new opportunities. Providing a wider range of services can attract clients looking for holistic financial solutions.

b. Specialized Industry Expertise

Develop expertise in specific industries or niches to differentiate yourself from competitors. Focus on sectors where you have experience or a keen interest, and leverage your skills to provide specialized fractional CFO services tailored to the unique needs of these industries. Specialization can make you a sought-after expert in your chosen field.

c. Training and Workshops

Share your knowledge and expertise by offering training sessions or workshops. This can be an additional revenue stream and a way to showcase your expertise to potential clients. Ensure that your training materials are comprehensive and provide practical insights that participants can apply to their businesses. Training and workshops also position you as a thought leader in your industry.

By expanding your fractional CFO business, outsourcing tasks, and diversifying your services, you can position yourself for sustained growth and success. Remember to assess the potential risks and rewards of each expansion strategy and continuously evaluate your business performance to ensure profitability and client satisfaction. Maintain effective communication channels and deliver exceptional customer service throughout your growth journey. These elements will help you build a strong reputation and attract new clients who will contribute to the future success of your fractional CFO business. With the right strategies in place, you can confidently scale your business and achieve your goals as a fractional CFO.

In the next chapter, we'll explore techniques for maintaining high-quality service as you scale, ensuring your clients remain satisfied and loyal. Let's continue this journey together and secure the long-term success of your fractional CFO business!

Chapter 10: Navigating Challenges and Sustaining Success

Running a fractional CFO business can be incredibly rewarding, but it also comes with its fair share of challenges. Being aware of these challenges and having strategies to overcome them is crucial for sustaining long-term success. Let's delve into some common challenges faced by fractional CFO businesses and explore effective strategies to tackle them.

Common Challenges Faced by Fractional CFO Businesses

1. Managing Workload and Time

As a fractional CFO, juggling multiple clients and projects simultaneously is part of the job. However, managing your workload effectively is essential to ensure timely and high-quality deliverables. Here are some strategies to help you stay on top of your tasks:

- **Use Project Management Tools:** Utilize project management software or apps to keep track of your tasks, deadlines, and progress on different projects. Tools like Trello, Asana, or Monday.com can be lifesavers in organizing your workflow.

- **Set Realistic Expectations:** Communicate clearly with your clients about project timelines and manage their expectations accordingly. Transparency about what can be achieved and by when will foster trust and reduce stress.

- **Delegate When Necessary:** Consider outsourcing certain tasks or partnering with other professionals to help lighten your workload. Delegating non-core tasks allows you to focus on high-value activities that require your expertise.

2. Staying Updated on Industry Trends and Regulations

The financial industry is constantly evolving with new trends, technologies, and regulations emerging regularly. Staying informed and up-to-date is crucial for providing the best service to your clients. Here are some tips for staying current:

- **Continuous Learning:** Stay updated on industry trends and changes by attending conferences, webinars, and workshops related to finance and accounting. These events offer valuable insights and networking opportunities.

- **Professional Development:** Take advantage of educational opportunities such as certifications, training programs, and online courses to enhance your knowledge and skills. Keeping your credentials current and relevant is vital.
- **Stay Connected:** Join professional associations and networks relevant to your field to stay connected with industry professionals and receive regular updates on the latest trends and regulations. Organizations like the AICPA or the IMA can be great resources.

3. Maintaining Client Relationships

Building and maintaining strong client relationships is essential for the success of your fractional CFO business. Here are some tips for effectively managing client relationships:

- **Regular Communication:** Maintain open lines of communication with your clients. Schedule regular check-ins and provide timely updates on their financial situation. Consistent communication builds trust and keeps clients informed.

- **Understand Their Business:**
  Continuously strive to understand your clients' businesses, their goals, and challenges. This will help you tailor your services to meet their specific needs and demonstrate your commitment to their success.
- **Be a Problem-Solver:** Proactively identify and address issues or potential risks your clients may face. Offer solutions and recommendations to help them overcome these challenges. Being seen as a trusted advisor will strengthen your client relationships.

Managing Workload and Time

Maintaining a healthy work-life balance is essential for long-term success as a fractional CFO. Here are some additional strategies to help you manage your workload and time effectively:

- **Prioritize Tasks:** Identify the most important and time-sensitive tasks and tackle them first. This will help you stay focused and maximize your productivity. Use prioritization techniques like the Eisenhower Matrix to categorize tasks by urgency and importance.
- **Time Blocking:** Block out specific chunks of time for different tasks and projects. This helps create structure and

ensures that you allocate enough time to each client. Time blocking can also help reduce distractions and improve focus.

- **Automate Processes:** Utilize technology and software to automate repetitive tasks such as data entry, report generation, and invoicing. Automation can save you valuable time and reduce the chances of errors. Tools like QuickBooks, Xero, and Excel macros can be incredibly helpful.

Sustaining Long-Term Success

To sustain long-term success as a fractional CFO, focus on delivering exceptional customer service and continuously improving your skills and abilities. Here are some tips to help you stay ahead:

- **Continuous Learning:** Stay updated on the latest industry trends, regulations, and best practices through ongoing education and professional development opportunities. Lifelong learning will keep you at the top of your game.
- **Seek Feedback:** Regularly seek feedback from your clients to ensure you are meeting their expectations and to identify areas for improvement. Constructive feedback can provide

valuable insights into how you can enhance your services.

- **Network:** Build and maintain a strong network of professionals in your field. Networking can lead to new clients, partnerships, and opportunities. Attend industry events, join professional groups, and engage with peers to expand your network.
- **Stay Adaptable:** Embrace change and be flexible in your approach. Continuously evaluate and adjust your strategies to stay relevant in a fast-paced business environment. Being adaptable will help you navigate changes in the market and client needs.
- **Focus on Client Satisfaction:** Place a strong emphasis on providing exceptional customer service. Satisfied clients are more likely to refer your services to others and become repeat clients. Go the extra mile to exceed client expectations and build lasting relationships.

By navigating challenges effectively, staying updated on industry trends and regulations, and maintaining strong client relationships, you can sustain long-term success as a fractional CFO. Remember to continuously strive for excellence in your work and adapt to the changing needs of your clients and the industry.